SMITH-DIST...
PR...

I MISS MY DAD

THE IMPORTANCE

OF A FATHER IN A SONS LIFE

Written by: Brian K. Smith

Table of Contents

Dedication

I am honored and privileged to have had such a wonderful father. He was always a constant source of love, support, and guidance throughout my life. His unwavering dedication to our family and his tireless work ethic has always been an inspiration to me. His wisdom and advice have been invaluable in helping me navigate the challenges of life. I am eternally grateful for the sacrifices he has made and the love he has shown me. I am truly blessed to have him as my father. I would like to take this opportunity to acknowledge his contributions and express my deepest gratitude.

I will forever love you, Dad.

Foreword

My life journey with Brian started in 1978 – I was seven years old. His grandfather married my grandmother that year, and their union sparked the bond between him and me. As a (Pittsburgh, PA) Westside kid from Greenway, I was also an "honorary member" of the Chartiers City Crew, the Westside Pittsburgh neighborhood Brian called home.

Brian and I made our way through our latter childhood, adolescent, and young adult years together. I had the privilege of growing and evolving as a young man with him. We experienced countless funny, frightful, painful, noble, shameful, and chivalrous adventures side-by-side. We have vivid memories where we stood tall in the face of life's challenges and when we failed to display character.

I had the honor of having Brian's parents – Mrs. Ida and Mr. Smitty – sow into my life in many, many, many meaningful ways. He and I are connected by life experiences and by the life lessons they deposited in us. I moved away from Pittsburgh after college, so distance has robbed Brian and I of frequent face-to-face conversations but not consistent communication, and we have certainly remained kindred spirits.

I am a father of four and a PaPa, including two sons and a grandson. Without question, I am a better father and PaPa because of my life journey with Brian and the example of the fatherhood of Mr. Smitty. With all that said, I can confirm the character and authenticity of this book's author. I can attest that the love, sacrifice, and model of consistent character of Mr. Smitty yielded much good fruit – Brian K. Smith as a Godly servant, faithful husband, and diligent father.

As you read through these pages, Brian shares his heart, words from Mr. Smitty's heart, and practical advice on how fathers or father figures can sow seeds of wisdom into their sons. A theme throughout the book is "model." Weaved into the chapters is the concept that fathers must consistently model behaviors and habits they desire their sons to emulate, a radical shift from the "do as I say, not as I do" paradigm many were raised in.

The book also inspires fathers to help sons understand the importance and value of integrity, honesty, hard work, and perseverance. Buying into the notions of working hard now to reap benefits later, not cutting corners if no one will notice, honoring commitments when it's inconvenient, not retaliating, etc., can be challenging for boys and young men. Fathers are critical in helping sons embrace these values as the key to long-term productivity and prosperity. This book will Bless you, your sons, your families, and your communities.

"Listen, my sons, to a father's instruction; pay attention and gain understanding. I give you sound learning, so do not forsake my teaching. For I too was a son to my father,

still tender, and cherished by my mother. Then he taught me, and said to me, "Take hold of my words with all your heart; keep my commandments, and you will live..."

(Proverbs 4:1-4)

-Billy Terry

Brian Smith and Billy Terry – 8th Grade Promotion Ceremony at Greenway Middle School (1985)

Introduction

Welcome to "I Missed My Dad: The Importance of a Father in a Boy's Life." This book is written to explore the critical role a father plays in shaping the life of a boy. From birth to adulthood, a father's presence, guidance, and love can have a profound impact on a boy's emotional, psychological, and social development.

The bond between a father and son is unique, and it is something that can shape a boy's entire life. A father is a role model, a mentor, a guide, and a protector. He teaches a boy how to be a man, how to navigate the world, and how to live a fulfilling life. A father's influence on a boy's self-esteem, confidence, and sense of identity is immeasurable.

In this book, we will explore the different ways in which a father can shape a boy's life. We will look at the different stages of a boy's development and the role a father plays in each stage. We will also look at the impact a father has on a boy's emotional and psychological well-being and the importance of a strong father-son bond.

This book is written for fathers, mothers, and anyone who wants to understand the importance of a father in a boy's life. It is my hope that it will inspire and empower fathers to be the best they can be for their sons and help them to understand the impact they have on their son's lives.

Thank you for joining me on this journey to explore the importance of a father in a boy's life. I hope you enjoy reading this book as much as I enjoyed writing it.

Chapter 1: The Role of a Father in a Boy's Development

The Indispensable Role of Fathers in Shaping Boys into Men

Throughout my years working with boys and their families, the profound influence of a father on a boy's development has consistently emerged as a pivotal theme. This chapter explores the multi-faceted role of fathers, emphasizing not just their contribution to emotional, social, and behavioral support but also the lasting impact of their involvement in their sons' lives.

Defining the Father's Role

A father's role extends beyond mere provision, encapsulating emotional guidance, quality time, discipline, and serving as a beacon of positive behavior. These elements are crucial in fostering a nurturing environment for a boy's holistic development.

The Importance of a Father's Influence

Research underscores the significant benefits boys reap from having an engaged father figure, including heightened self-esteem, improved mental health, and reduced behavioral issues. Fathers often impart a unique blend of encouragement and challenge, essential for developing assertiveness, self-control, and resilience.

Fathers as Role Models and Mentors

Beyond emotional support, fathers are pivotal in modeling healthy masculinity and identity. Witnessing fathers engage in respectful interactions, express emotions constructively, and participate in diverse activities encourages boys to adopt similar behaviors, shaping their perceptions of masculinity in inclusive ways.

Addressing the Gap: Role Models Beyond Fathers

Acknowledging the reality that not all boys have present fathers, the importance of alternative male role models becomes clear. Grandfathers, uncles, coaches, and mentors can equally contribute to a boy's development, offering guidance and support where needed.

The Lifelong Role of Fathers

The influence of a father does not wane with childhood but continues to be significant throughout a boy's life into adulthood. This enduring support plays a pivotal role in shaping a boy's journey into manhood.

Challenging Misconceptions

Contrary to the view that a father's primary role is as a provider, it is their emotional involvement that holds paramount importance in a boy's development. Active fatherhood is linked to better academic performance, healthier peer relationships, and a lower propensity for risky behaviors among boys.

Practical Steps for Fathers

Engaging actively in their sons' lives, fathers can foster a positive development environment through quality time, attentive listening, guidance, and by exemplifying healthy behaviors and attitudes.

The Personal Touch: A Father's Legacy

My own experience with my father, a passionate car enthusiast, exemplifies the profound impact of shared activities on a boy's development. Weekends spent in the garage, mastering the intricacies of automotive care, not only equipped me with valuable skills but also shaped my work ethic, pride in my accomplishments, and a deep-seated sense of responsibility. These lessons, ingrained during those formative years, have been instrumental in my journey to adulthood.

Conclusion

The role of a father, or a father figure, is undeniably critical in a boy's development. Through emotional support, positive role modeling, and practical guidance, fathers lay the groundwork for their sons to grow into well-rounded, resilient men. My story is but one of many, illustrating the lasting impact of a father's influence on a boy's path to becoming a man.

Chapter 2: A Father's Influence on a Boy's Self-Esteem

The Foundations of Self-Esteem: A Father's Influence

Self-esteem, the bedrock of a person's mental and emotional well-being, reflects one's self-worth and confidence in their abilities. It is a cornerstone of happiness, satisfaction, and motivation and is crucial for mental health. This chapter delves into how fathers play a pivotal role in nurturing and elevating their sons' self-esteem.

Understanding Self-Esteem

At its core, self-esteem is about recognizing one's value and believing in one's capabilities. It influences nearly every aspect of our lives, from how we operate in our careers to the health of our relationships.

The Role of Fathers in Building Self-Esteem

Research unequivocally shows that fathers significantly impact their sons' self-esteem. Boys with positive father relationships often exhibit higher self-worth levels than those without such figures in their lives. This positive influence stems from several key areas:

- Emotional Support: Fathers who provide warmth, nurture, and support foster a sense of being valued in their sons. This emotional foundation is critical for developing a positive self-image.

- Guidance and Structure: Discipline and structure from fathers help sons develop competence and mastery, which are vital for self-esteem. Boys who feel capable of overcoming challenges and making wise decisions gain confidence in their abilities.
- Healthy Masculinity: Fathers modeling respectful behavior, emotional expression, and engagement in diverse activities offer sons a broader, more positive perspective on masculinity that is crucial for their self-concept.

The Long-term Impact

The influence of a father extends into adulthood, shaping a son's mental health outcomes, relationship success, and professional achievements. Positive father-son relationships lay a groundwork that benefits sons throughout their lives.

Alternative Role Models

Acknowledging that not all boys have positive father figures, the presence of other male role models like grandfathers, uncles, or mentors remains invaluable. These figures can fill critical roles in helping boys develop a robust sense of self-worth and confidence.

Strategies for Fathers

Building self-esteem in sons can be approached in various ways, including:

Quality Time: Engaging in shared activities strengthens the father-son bond.

Emotional Support: Warmth and support from fathers assure sons of their value and belonging.

Guidance and Structure: Providing clear expectations and constructive feedback helps sons build competence and confidence.

Modeling Healthy Behaviors: Fathers who exhibit healthy emotional expression and respect help sons develop positive self-views.

A Personal Reflection

Reflecting on my own journey, my father's steadfast belief in my potential was a beacon during my formative years. Facing academic challenges, his encouragement transformed my outlook, teaching me that with belief and effort, I can surpass my limitations. This lesson in self-belief, instilled through my father's support, has been a guiding light in my life. One specific instance that stands out to me was when I was in elementary school and struggling with math class. There was a test coming up, and I didn't think I could pass. But my father sat me down and told me, "You can do this. I believe in you." He helped me study and understand the material, and I ended up getting an A.

That experience taught me that I can accomplish anything I set my mind to, as long as I believe in myself and have someone there to support and encourage me. I am forever grateful for my father's guidance and support.

Conclusion

Fathers wield a profound influence on their sons' development of self-esteem. Through emotional support, guidance, and modeling healthy attitudes, they lay a foundation for their sons' lifelong confidence and success. My own experiences attest to this enduring impact, underscoring the invaluable role fathers play in their sons' lives.

Chapter 3: The Importance of a Father's Love and Affection

The Transformative Power of a Father's Love

For fathers, one of the most profound ways to impact our children's lives is through the expression of love and affection. While seemingly fundamental, the depth of a father's love is pivotal to a child's emotional and psychological development.

The Importance of a Father's Love

Creating Emotional Security

A father's love lays the foundation for a child's sense of security and stability. Feeling cherished by their father equips children with confidence and resilience, which is essential for navigating life's ups and downs.

Promoting Healthy Emotional Development

Consistent, nurturing love from a father plays a crucial role in children's emotional growth, contributing to a robust sense of self-worth and long-term mental well-being.

Strengthening Bonds

Love fortifies the father-child relationship, fostering a durable connection that persists through the transition from childhood to adulthood.

Expressing Love: Challenges and Strategies

Recognizing that expressing affection doesn't always come naturally, especially for those who may not have experienced it firsthand, is crucial. Here are strategies to help bridge the gap:

- Physical Affection: Simple gestures like hugs and gentle touches convey care and warmth effectively.
- Quality Time: Dedicate moments to engage in shared interests or simply to converse, reinforcing your love through attention and involvement.
- Verbal Praise and Affirmation: Articulate your love and pride openly, celebrating your child's unique qualities and achievements.
- Active Listening and Presence: Being attentively available and listening to your child's thoughts and feelings signals profound love and respect.
- Seeking Support: It's okay to seek external support if expressing affection proves challenging. Consulting therapists or connecting with fellow fathers can offer valuable perspectives and strategies.

A Personal Reflection on Affection

Reflecting on my own upbringing, I cherish the affection my father demonstrated, albeit in his understated way. A simple memory of playing basketball together in the park encapsulates his way of expressing care—through quality time and shared activities. These moments, though modest, profoundly impacted my understanding of love and connection. One of my fondest memories is of my father taking me to the park to play basketball. We would spend hours shooting hoops and talking about life. Even though we were just playing a simple game, it meant the world to me because it was a way for my father to connect with me and show me that he cared. My father's affection taught me

the importance of expressing love and caring for others. I strive to be as affectionate and supportive as he was.

Conclusion

The act of expressing love and affection is a cornerstone of fatherhood, with the power to shape a child's future profoundly. It goes beyond mere emotional expression, serving as a critical component of their development and the bond they share. Like the memories of basketball with my father, it's these expressions of love that leave a lasting imprint on a child's heart, guiding them as they navigate their own journeys.

Chapter 4: A Father's Impact on a Boy's Social Skills

Fathers' Influence on Sons' Social Skills: Insights from the Little League Field

In my role as a little league football coach, I've observed the profound impact fathers have on their sons' social development. Fathers play a pivotal role in shaping their sons' abilities to interact positively with others, navigate complex social settings, and develop emotional intelligence.

Fathers as Role Models for Social Behavior

Modeling Social Skills

Fathers are key role models for their sons. By displaying empathy, respect, and kindness, they set a standard for their sons to emulate in their own interactions.

Encouraging Social Engagement

Promoting Social Interactions

Fathers who foster strong bonds with their sons can boost their confidence in social settings. Encouraging sons to build friendships and partake in group activities enhances their social skills and self-assurance.

Building Emotional Intelligence

Developing Awareness and Expression

Fathers are instrumental in helping their sons understand and manage emotions, a critical aspect of social competence. Engaging in conversations about feelings and demonstrating healthy emotional expression are key.

Guidance Through Social Challenges

Navigating Relationships and Conflicts

As boys confront the intricate social dynamics of school and hobbies, fathers' guidance and support can help them forge healthy relationships and approach conflicts constructively.

Fostering Independence and Confidence

Encouraging Autonomy

Support and encouragement from fathers are crucial for fostering independence, which is integral to social growth. A self-assured son is more adept at forming positive relationships and handling social situations.

The Impact of Fathers: Statistical Insights

Research underscores the significant influence of fathers in developing their sons' social skills:

- Warm and Involved Fathers: Studies in the Journal of Family Psychology highlight that children with affectionate, engaged fathers show enhanced social skills, particularly in forming positive peer relationships.

- Fathers and Emotional Intelligence: Research indicates that sons of fathers who provide emotional support and model emotional intelligence exhibit heightened emotional awareness and regulation skills.

- Navigating Social Situations: Fathers who discuss peer pressure and offer guidance aid their sons in effectively handling social situations and resisting negative influences, as per studies in the Journal of Youth and Adolescence.

- Positive Feedback and Praise: Findings from the Journal of Child and Family Studies suggest that fathers who offer warm support and positive reinforcement can significantly improve their sons' social abilities.

A Coach's Perspective

Drawing on my experience, I've seen the tangible benefits of fathers' involvement in their sons' lives. The football field is not just a place for physical activity but a microcosm where social skills are honed, often reflecting the influence of a father's love, guidance, and support.

Conclusion

The role of a father in developing a child's social skills cannot be overstated. From modeling positive behaviors to providing emotional guidance and fostering independence, fathers equip their sons with the tools needed for successful social interactions. This chapter underlines the profound and lasting impact fathers have on their sons' ability to navigate the complex social landscapes of life.

My dad played a significant role in shaping my social skills. He signed me up for sports teams, cub scouts, and other groups that forced me to interact with other kids. At first, it was difficult for me, but as I got to know my teammates and classmates, I started to feel more comfortable and confident in social situations. My father also taught me the importance of being a good listener and showing empathy towards others. He would often tell me, "It's not just about what you say, it's about how you make others feel." This helped me understand the value of building strong relationships and the importance of treating others with kindness and respect. I believe that his teachings have helped me develop strong social skills and become a more confident, outgoing person.

A father's impact on his son's social skills can be profound. By modeling positive social behaviors, encouraging socialization, building emotional intelligence, providing guidance and support, and fostering independence and autonomy, fathers can help their sons develop the social skills and confidence they need to navigate the challenges of childhood and beyond.

Chapter 5: A Father's Guidance in a Boy's Education and Career Choices

A Father's Role in Shaping Educational and Career Paths

As a father, guiding and supporting my son through the maze of educational and career choices stands as one of my most significant responsibilities. The pathway a child takes in education and career is influenced by numerous factors, but a father's active involvement can be pivotal in guiding boys to make informed decisions and follow their passions.

Influencing Educational and Career Choices

Support and Encouragement

The foundation of a child's academic and career success often lies in feeling supported and encouraged by their parents. Fathers play a vital role in this aspect, be it through attending school functions, aiding with homework, or showing genuine interest in their son's hobbies and educational pursuits.

Identifying Interests and Strengths

Guidance from fathers is invaluable in helping sons recognize their interests and strengths. Engaging in conversations, providing feedback, and creating opportunities for exploration can aid boys in discovering their passions and honing the skills necessary for their desired careers.

Fostering a Love for Lifelong Learning

Education is not confined to the classroom; it's an enduring journey. Fathers can instill a lifelong love of learning by exhibiting curiosity, sharing reading experiences, and encouraging the exploration of new ideas and subjects.

Guidance on Key Decisions

As sons face significant decisions like selecting a college or a career path, fathers can offer essential guidance. This might include collaborative research, discussing various options' advantages and disadvantages, or simply listening as their sons contemplate their choices.

Valuing Hard Work and Perseverance

Imparting the significance of hard work, perseverance, and resilience is critical for success in any field. Fathers who exemplify these values and encourage the same in their sons lay the groundwork for their children to develop the grit necessary to achieve their aspirations.

Strategies for Fathers

While each father-son relationship is distinct, several universal approaches can aid in guiding a child's educational and career journey:

- Be Present and Engaged: The key to effective guidance is active presence and engagement in your son's life. This includes quality time spent together, showing interest in his academic and personal interests, and being involved in his life choices.

- Encourage Exploration: Facilitate learning and discovery by exposing sons to diverse academic and career opportunities. This could involve museum visits, attending educational events, or engaging in discussions about various subjects.

- Provide Support and Insight: Offer support and insight during pivotal decision-making moments. This can range from research assistance to providing thoughtful advice or simply being an empathetic listener.

- Cultivate a Passion for Learning: Demonstrate a love for learning and encourage your son to delve into new topics and ideas. This enthusiasm for knowledge can be a powerful motivator and a cornerstone for future success.

- Celebrate Successes and Embrace Failures: Help your son build resilience by celebrating his achievements and learning from setbacks. This approach fosters a balanced perspective on success and failure, crucial for long-term personal and professional growth.

Conclusion

The role of a father in guiding educational and career pathways is multi-faceted and deeply impactful. By providing support, encouraging exploration, and fostering key life skills, fathers can significantly influence their sons' academic and professional journeys. This guidance not only shapes their immediate educational choices but also lays a strong foundation for their future career success and personal fulfillment.

Chapter 6: The Father-Son Bond and Its Impact on Emotional Health

The Vital Role of the Father-Son Bond in Emotional Health

The bond between a father and his son is a unique and potent connection that is foundational for a boy's emotional health. This bond, built on trust, love, and mutual respect, is instrumental in shaping a boy's journey through childhood and adolescence.

Impact on Emotional Health

Building Self-Esteem and Confidence

A father's love and support are crucial in fostering a child's self-esteem and confidence. Feeling valued and accepted by their father, a child is more likely to develop a positive self-image and a strong sense of self-worth.

Emotional Stability and Security

The father-son relationship offers emotional stability and security. Knowing they can rely on their father's love and support, children are better equipped to handle anxiety and stress, feeling safer and more secure in their environment.

Encouraging Healthy Emotional Expression

Fathers play a key role in encouraging their sons to express emotions healthily. By modeling effective communication and emotional regulation, fathers can guide their sons in developing emotional intelligence and resilience.

Fostering Healthy Relationships

A strong father-son bond aids in the development of healthy relationships. Learning trust and reliability from their fathers, boys are more likely to form relationships based on trust, respect, and open communication.

Strengthening the Father-Son Bond: Challenges and Strategies

While building a robust father-son bond is rewarding, it can come with its challenges. Here are strategies to help strengthen this relationship:

Be Present and Engaged: Being actively present in your son's life is critical. This involves quality time, interest in his hobbies and pursuits, and being available for support.

Model Healthy Emotional Expression: Fathers should demonstrate healthy emotional expression, sharing vulnerabilities and guiding their sons in expressing their emotions constructively.

Unconditional Love and Acceptance: Offering unconditional love and acceptance reassures children of their value, regardless of their achievements or failures.

Guidance and Boundaries: Providing guidance and setting boundaries are essential. This includes setting clear expectations and supporting your son in developing responsibility and accountability.

Celebrate Successes, Learn from Failures: Encouraging a growth mindset by celebrating successes and learning from failures builds resilience and emotional intelligence.

The Power of Emotional Support and Guidance

The emotional support and guidance a father provides are invaluable. They foster a strong sense of self-worth and resilience, equipping sons to face life's challenges. Additionally, fathers can be role models, teaching their sons to cope with difficult emotions and handle life's complexities.

Developing Social and Communication Skills

Fathers also aid in developing their sons' social and communication skills. Engaging in activities and conversations, fathers can guide their sons in effective self-expression, relationship-building, and navigating social situations.

Acknowledging Challenges in the Father-Son Relationship

Not all father-son relationships are positive. In cases of absence or emotional unavailability, sons might struggle with feelings of rejection and low self-esteem. It's crucial for fathers to understand the impact of their presence and actions and strive for a healthy, nurturing relationship. I often struggled with feelings of insecurity and self-doubt. But my father was always there to support me and provide guidance. One of the ways my father helped me was by simply being there for me. He would listen to me when I needed to talk and offer words of encouragement when I was feeling down. Having someone to turn to who truly cared about my well-being was incredibly important. My father also helped me to develop a strong sense of self-worth. He would often remind me that I was capable and deserving of success, even when I was struggling to believe

in myself. His belief in me helped me to believe in myself too and it was instrumental in my journey to adulthood.

Conclusion

The father-son bond is a cornerstone for emotional health, offering stability, love, and support. By nurturing this relationship, fathers can help their sons develop emotional intelligence, resilience, and the ability to lead fulfilling lives. This bond is not just a source of support but a guiding force in a son's life, empowering him to navigate the complexities of the world with confidence and grace.

Chapter 7: A Father's Influence on a Boy's Moral and Ethical Development

The Essential Role of Fathers in Shaping Moral and Ethical Values

As fathers, one of our most significant responsibilities is to guide our children, especially sons, in developing a strong moral and ethical compass. While both parents contribute immensely to this process, fathers often exert a unique influence on a boy's understanding of right and wrong, values, and decision-making.

Modeling Good Behavior

Living by Example

Children learn by observing, and as fathers, our actions speak louder than our words. To instill virtues like honesty, hard work, and respect in our sons, we must embody these qualities ourselves. Our behavior sets a template for them to emulate.

Setting Expectations and Boundaries

The Importance of Rules and Consequences

Establishing clear rules and consistent, fair consequences helps sons understand the significance of boundaries.

Explaining the rationale behind these rules is equally important, fostering an understanding of why they matter.

Being a Pillar of Support

Open Communication and Understanding

One of the most impactful ways we can aid our sons' moral and ethical growth is by being available and supportive. Creating an environment where they can share their dilemmas and thoughts without fear of judgment is crucial for their moral reasoning development.

Sharing Personal Experiences

Learning from Life Lessons

Sharing our life stories, including our triumphs and failures, offers real-life context to moral and ethical lessons. Discussing the repercussions of our choices helps sons grasp the complexities of ethical decision-making.

Teaching Empathy and Compassion

Fostering Care for Others

Instilling empathy and compassion in our sons is vital. By demonstrating care for others and understanding different perspectives, we encourage our sons to develop these crucial emotional skills.

Embracing Imperfection

Learning from Mistakes

Acknowledging our own imperfections and mistakes and showing accountability for them teaches a valuable lesson. It's important for sons to understand that making mistakes is part of being human, and owning up to them is integral to moral integrity.

Conclusion

The influence of a father on a son's moral and ethical development cannot be understated. Through our actions, guidance, and the values we demonstrate, we have the profound opportunity to shape our sons into ethical, responsible, and compassionate individuals. Our role is not just to instruct but to inspire and equip them with the moral tools they need to navigate the complexities of life.

Chapter 8: The Father-Son Relationship and Its Impact on Mental Health

The Impact of the Father-Son Relationship on Mental Health

In my experience as a youth football coach, I have observed the substantial impact the father-son relationship has on young boys' mental health. Fathers are pivotal in shaping their sons' emotional development, influencing their self-esteem, sense of security, and overall mental well-being.

The Importance of Emotional Bonding

Creating a Secure Emotional Base

A strong emotional bond between father and son fosters confidence, high self-esteem, and a feeling of security. This relationship serves as a safe foundation from which boys can confidently explore the world.

Challenges of Weak Emotional Bonds

Conversely, the absence of a strong emotional connection can lead to feelings of insecurity, anxiety, and low self-esteem. This lack of connection may result in a sense of disconnection from family and community, fostering isolation and loneliness.

Modeling Positive Behaviors and Attitudes

Impact of Positive Role Modeling

Boys raised by emotionally supportive, kind, and empathetic fathers are more likely to develop these traits. As children imitate their parents, positive behaviors exhibited at home are often internalized and emulated.

Consequences of Negative Role Modeling

Boys exposed to emotionally distant, critical, or aggressive fathers may face mental health challenges, including anxiety, depression, and even substance abuse. Such environments can lead to feelings of being unloved or unsupported.

Developing Healthy Coping Mechanisms

Building Resilience

Fathers can guide their sons in developing effective coping strategies for stress and anxiety. Modeling healthy behaviors and encouraging engagement in constructive activities can help sons build resilience against life's challenges.

Fostering a Sense of Purpose and Meaning

Encouraging Passions and Interests

Fathers who encourage their sons to pursue their interests and passions help them develop a sense of identity and purpose. This sense of direction is a protective factor against various mental health issues.

Research Insights on the Father-Son Relationship

- Several studies highlight the importance of the father-son relationship in mental health:

- Positive Father Involvement: Research in the Journal of Youth and Adolescence indicates that sons with involved fathers have better mental health, showing lower levels of depression and anxiety.

- Effective Father-Son Communication: A study in the Journal of Child and Family Studies links positive father-son communication with improved mental health for both, including reduced stress and higher self-esteem.

- Impact of Father-Son Conflict: High levels of conflict, as per the Journal of Marriage and Family, correlate with increased depression and anxiety in both fathers and sons.

- Long-Term Effects: According to the Journal of Family Psychology, the quality of the father-son relationship in childhood influences mental health outcomes in adulthood, with positive relationships leading to lower levels of depression and anxiety.

Conclusion

The father-son relationship is a crucial determinant of a young boy's mental health. Positive engagement, emotional support, and constructive communication from fathers can significantly enhance their sons' mental well-being. My observations in youth football, coupled with research findings, underscore the vital role fathers play in their sons' emotional and mental development. Through nurturing a strong, healthy father-son relationship, we can foster a generation of boys with better mental health and emotional resilience.

Chapter 9: A Father's Role in Teaching a Boy About Manhood and Responsibility

Guiding a Son into Manhood: A Father's Crucial Role

As a father, I recognize my profound responsibility in shaping my son's understanding of manhood and instilling in him a sense of responsibility. My guidance is integral in helping him develop a positive sense of self and in preparing him for adulthood's challenges.

Teaching Responsibility

Fostering Accountability and Ownership

One of the essential lessons I can impart is the concept of responsibility. This involves teaching my son to own his actions, acknowledge his mistakes, and understand the value of hard work and perseverance. By demonstrating responsibility and enforcing accountability, I aim to cultivate a strong sense of personal duty in him.

Modeling Manhood

Providing a Positive and Healthy Role Model

In today's society, where conflicting notions of manhood abound, my role as a father is to offer a positive and healthy example. I strive to teach my son values like honesty, integrity, respect, empathy, and kindness, and model these in my interactions with others.

Developing a Positive Self-Image

Embracing Strengths and Weaknesses

Helping my son build a positive self-image is crucial. This means encouraging him to appreciate his own worth, recognize his strengths and weaknesses, and understand the importance of physical health and healthy habits.

Nurturing Healthy Relationships

Teaching Communication and Respect

A significant part of manhood is understanding healthy relationships. I teach my son the importance of communication, trust, respect, and appreciation in relationships. By modeling behaviors like active listening and conflict resolution, I guide him in navigating relational challenges.

Navigating Life's Path

Guiding Educational and Career Choices

Beyond manhood and responsibility, I play a vital role in helping my son make informed decisions about his education and career. I support him in exploring various paths, pursuing his interests, and developing essential skills like communication and problem-solving.

Providing Emotional Support

Supporting him through adolescence and young adulthood involves offering emotional support during tough times and helping him develop healthy coping mechanisms for stress and anxiety father played a pivotal role in teaching me about manhood and responsibility provided guidance and mentorship that helped shape my understanding of what it means to be a responsible and respected man. One of the things my father taught me was the importance of hard work. He would often tell me, "A real man takes care of his responsibilities and works hard to provide for his family." He instilled in me the value of hard work and the importance of being a reliable and dependable person.

My father also taught me about the importance of being a good role model. He would often say, "Be the kind of man you would want your own son to be." This taught me to strive to be the best version of myself and to lead by example.

In addition, my father taught me about the importance of self-discipline and self-control. He would often remind me that "A real man has the discipline to control his thoughts, emotions, and actions." This helped me to develop self-discipline and self-control, which are essential qualities for any man.

Conclusion

The role of a father in guiding a son into manhood and teaching him about responsibility and life navigation is critical. By providing guidance, support, and positive examples, I am committed to helping my son grow into a well-rounded, successful adult. This journey is not just about imparting knowledge but also about nurturing his growth, understanding his individuality, and preparing him for the complexities of the world.

Chapter 10: The Lasting Legacy of a Father's Impact on a Boy's Life

The Enduring Legacy of a Father's Influence

As a father, the influence I have on my son transcends the bounds of our immediate interactions. The values I instill, the lessons I teach, and the model of manhood I provide will shape his character and choices for a lifetime. This lasting impact underscores the gravity of my role and the legacy I am crafting.

Role Modeling and Value Instillation

Shaping Character through Actions

As my son's primary role model, my actions and behaviors are pivotal in shaping his own. Demonstrating respect, kindness, and honesty sets a standard for him to emulate. Conversely, exhibiting negative behaviors poses the risk of them being mirrored. Understanding this dynamic guides my conduct, ensuring I embody the virtues I hope to see in him.

Teaching Manhood and Responsibility

Preparing for Life's Challenges

Imparting values such as hard work, honesty, and accountability prepares my son for the complexities of adulthood. Teaching respect for others and the importance of positive contributions to society equips him to be a responsible and active member of the community. These lessons form the bedrock of his development into a conscientious adult.

Beyond Childhood: A Lasting Influence

The Legacy of Fatherhood

The impact of my role as a father endures well beyond my son's childhood. The values and traditions instilled in him will likely influence his actions as an adult, potentially being passed down to his own children. This ripple effect of my parenting underscores the significance of each lesson and interaction.

Preserving and Honoring Family Heritage

Connecting Through Stories

My father taught me about our family's legacy through storytelling, recounting our ancestors' trials and triumphs. These narratives instilled in me a deep appreciation for our heritage and the importance of preserving it. He often emphasized our responsibility to carry forward our ancestors' legacy, impressing upon me the duty to honor and extend our family history to future generations.

Conclusion

The role of a father in a son's life is profound, with implications that reach far beyond their immediate relationship. As a father, I am a role model, a teacher, and a guardian of our family's legacy. The values, lessons, and traditions I impart will shape my son's character and choices throughout his life and may continue to resonate through future generations. This enduring legacy is a powerful testament to the significance of fatherhood.

There is No Manual for Fatherhood

The journey of fatherhood, often perceived as a path without a manual, is a testament to its intricate and personalized nature. As we progress into chapters 11-20, it's crucial to remember that fatherhood extends beyond biological ties, encompassing diverse roles men play in nurturing and guiding children and young people.

The Impact of Fatherhood

A Lasting Influence on Child Development

Fatherhood profoundly affects a child's development, with far-reaching implications. Research consistently shows that children with engaged fathers exhibit higher self-esteem, superior social skills, and enhanced educational outcomes. They are also less inclined to indulge in risky behaviors like substance abuse or criminal activities.

The Uniqueness of Every Father-Son Relationship

No Standardized Approach to Fathering

One of the pivotal challenges of fatherhood is its resistance to a standardized approach. Every father-son bond is distinct, and strategies that succeed in one family might not resonate in another. This reality underscores the absence of a definitive "owner manual" for fatherhood.

Diverse Forms of Fatherhood

Multiple Facets of a Father's Role

Fatherhood manifests in various forms - from biological fathers to stepfathers, foster fathers, and surrogate fathers. Each, irrespective of the nature of their role, significantly influences a child's life.

The Journey of Fatherhood

Navigating Personalized Pathways

Fatherhood is a journey marked by continuous learning and adaptation. It's about discovering what resonates best with your family, being receptive to change as children evolve, and understanding that there's no singular correct way to father.

Keys to Successful Fathering

Open Communication and Patience

Effective fatherhood hinges on open and honest communication. Engaging actively in your child's life, listening attentively, and providing support when needed are cornerstones of successful parenting. Patience and understanding are also vital, recognizing that children, like all of us, learn from their mistakes.

Conclusion

While there is no definitive manual for fatherhood, this does not imply a lack of guidance. Embracing the journey with awareness and commitment to your role can pave the way to being the best father possible. The chapters ahead aim to shed light on the essentials that can guide fathers through this fulfilling yet complex journey.

Chapter 11: How to Be Self-Sufficient and Independent

Fostering Self-Sufficiency and Independence in Young Athletes

As a youth football coach, I've witnessed the transformative power of sports in teaching young boys essential life skills. Beyond tactics and physical prowess, the invaluable lessons of self-sufficiency and independence stand out, shaping players into resilient and capable individuals.

The Essence of Self-Sufficiency and Independence

Cultivating Personal Responsibility

Self-sufficiency involves managing one's affairs, from finances to daily responsibilities, while independence focuses on emotional resilience and self-validation. These qualities are cornerstones of success, influencing personal and professional growth.

Implementing Life Lessons through Sports

Teaching Accountability

Encouraging players to own their actions and learn from mistakes fosters a culture of accountability. This approach helps them understand the value of self-reliance and the significance of navigating life's challenges with autonomy.

Goal Setting and Self-Motivation

Promoting goal-oriented behavior and self-motivation enhances players' work ethic and ambition. These skills are vital in pursuing personal and team objectives, mirroring the pursuit of life goals outside the sporting arena.

Modeling the Way

Leading by Example

As a coach, embodying self-sufficiency and independence serves as a powerful teaching tool. Demonstrating these qualities in managing team dynamics and personal challenges provides a real-life blueprint for young athletes to follow.

Practical Steps for Parents

Encouraging Household Responsibilities

Assigning chores and responsibilities fosters a sense of capability and accountability. Tasks like laundry, cooking, and tidying up teach valuable life management skills.

Promoting Exploration and Resilience

Encouraging your son to embrace new experiences and face challenges builds problem-solving abilities and resilience.

Such experiences are critical in developing a well-rounded and adaptable individual.

Setting and Managing Expectations

Understanding that success is not guaranteed in every endeavor teaches valuable lessons in perseverance and growth from failure. Encouraging persistence despite setbacks fosters a resilient mindset.

Offering Support with Autonomy

While promoting independence, it's crucial to provide a supportive backdrop. Offering guidance when necessary, without overstepping, balances the encouragement of independence with the assurance of support.

Being a Role Model

Your actions speak volumes. Demonstrating self-sufficiency and making informed, responsible decisions in your life sets a tangible example for your son to emulate.

Conclusion

The journey to instilling self-sufficiency and independence in young boys is multi-faceted, requiring patience, persistence, and thoughtful guidance. By incorporating these lessons into coaching and parenting practices, we can equip our young athletes with the skills they need to navigate adulthood successfully. The legacy of these teachings will not only enhance their immediate sporting endeavors but also prepare them for the broader challenges of life, ensuring they grow into confident, self-reliant adults

.

Chapter 12: The Importance of Integrity and Honesty

Cultivating Integrity and Honesty: A Father's Guide

As a father deeply invested in my son's moral development, I prioritize instilling the values of integrity and honesty. These foundational virtues are not just ideals but practical principles guiding personal and professional success and fostering meaningful relationships.

The Essence of Integrity and Honesty

Living by One's Values

Integrity and honesty entail a steadfast adherence to truth and a commitment to living in alignment with one's values. This includes the courage to speak truthfully, the resolve to act justly, and the reliability to fulfill one's commitments.

Teaching Through Everyday Actions

Encouraging Accountability from a Young Age

The journey of teaching integrity begins with everyday moments. Holding a child accountable for his actions in a compassionate yet firm manner lays the groundwork for understanding the significance of truthfulness and responsibility.

Modeling Values in Action

Being an Exemplar of Virtue

A father's actions profoundly influence his son's perception and adoption of integrity and honesty. Demonstrating these virtues through acknowledging one's mistakes, keeping promises, and treating others with respect serves as a powerful model for a young boy.

Engaging in Meaningful Conversations

Explaining the Importance of Virtues

Discussing the pivotal role of integrity and honesty in building trust, making ethical decisions, and achieving life's goals helps a son grasp the practical implications of these values. Concrete examples and personal anecdotes can illuminate their significance in real-life scenarios.

Reinforcing Positive Behaviors

Acknowledging Acts of Honesty and Integrity

Praising and celebrating instances where your son shows integrity and honesty reinforces the desirability of these traits. Positive reinforcement encourages a consistent demonstration of these values.

Navigating Challenges

Guiding Through a Complex World

In a society where dishonesty can often be observed, emphasizing the importance of integrity and honesty poses its challenges. Yet, through consistent demonstration, open dialogue, and celebration of virtuous actions, a father can imbue his son with a deep-rooted sense of these critical values.

Conclusion

The role of a father in nurturing integrity and honesty in his son is both a privilege and a responsibility. By embodying these values, engaging in open discussions about their importance, and reinforcing positive behaviors, a father lays a solid foundation for his son's moral development. This guidance is pivotal in helping a son navigate life with a strong moral compass, ensuring he grows into a man of character and virtue.

Chapter 13: The Value of Hard Work and Perseverance

Fostering a Strong Work Ethic and Perseverance in Children

Instilling a robust work ethic and a sense of perseverance in my child ranks high among my priorities as a father. These values have been instrumental in my life, and I firmly believe they will play a pivotal role in my child's journey to success.

The Importance of Hard Work and Perseverance

Foundation for Success

Success is often the fruit of diligent effort and commitment. Achieving goals, whether academic, athletic, or professional, typically demands significant time and dedication.

Navigating Life's Challenges

Life invariably presents challenges, from academic hurdles to professional setbacks. Perseverance empowers us to confront these obstacles head-on and emerge stronger.

Character Development

Beyond their practical benefits, hard work and perseverance are vital character traits, fostering responsibility, dependability, and self-discipline.

Strategies for Developing These Qualities

Modeling Virtue

Children absorb much from observing their parents. Demonstrating hard work in your endeavors and persevering through difficulties sets a powerful example for your child to emulate.

Valuing Effort Over Results

While celebrating achievements is crucial, acknowledging and praising effort is equally important. Recognizing your child's hard work reinforces the significance of perseverance, regardless of the outcome.

Creating Opportunities for Growth

Children need opportunities to practice perseverance and hard work. Encouraging them to tackle challenges and pursue their passions provides a practical context for developing these qualities.

Allowing Natural Consequences

Protecting our children from every hardship does them a disservice. Instead, supporting them through challenges without immediate rescue teaches valuable lessons in resilience and independence.

Goal Setting and Incremental Achievement

Big goals can feel daunting. Teaching children to break objectives into manageable steps fosters a sense of progress and maintains motivation, celebrating each milestone along the way.

Instilling the Virtue of Persistence

Highlighting the importance of continuing efforts despite difficulties is crucial. Discussing strategies for maintaining focus and motivation can equip your child to persevere through tough times.

Conclusion

Hard work and perseverance are not just pathways to success; they are virtues that shape character and resilience. By setting a positive example, encouraging effort, providing growth opportunities, allowing children to face challenges, teaching goal-setting skills, and emphasizing persistence, we can guide our children toward becoming hardworking and perseverant individuals. This journey requires patience and dedication from both the child and the parent, but the rewards—self-reliance, determination, and success—are immeasurable.

Chapter 14: How to Manage Money and Make Wise Financial Decisions

Empowering Children with Financial Wisdom: A Father's Guide

Understanding the value of money and making informed financial decisions are critical skills for navigating life's challenges. As a father, I've recognized the importance of teaching my children these skills early on, preparing them for a future of financial responsibility and independence.

Instilling the Value of Money

Earning Through Effort

It's crucial for children to grasp that money is earned through work and effort. Introducing age-appropriate tasks that allow them to earn money, such as household chores or helping neighbors, lays the foundation for this understanding.

Teaching Budgeting Basics

Needs vs. Wants

Educating children on distinguishing between needs and wants, prioritizing expenses, and resisting impulsive purchases is essential. Guiding them in managing their allowance and earnings teaches them to allocate funds responsibly: saving, spending on necessities, and sparingly using money for leisure.

The Power of Saving

Goal-Setting and Satisfaction

Encouraging children to save towards specific goals, whether for a toy or future aspirations like a car, instills the habit of saving and highlights the satisfaction of achieving financial goals through patience and discipline.

Understanding Debt

Good Debt vs. Bad Debt

Teaching the difference between beneficial debts (like mortgages or student loans) and detrimental debts (such as credit card debt) is vital. Children should learn to avoid bad debt and consider good debt cautiously, understanding its potential to either enhance or diminish financial health.

Credit Education

Credit Scores and Responsible Use

Explaining the mechanics of credit, the importance of a good credit score, and responsible credit card use is fundamental. Teaching them to pay off balances in full and warning against the pitfalls of high-interest debt are key lessons in credit management.

Involvement in Family Finances

Participating in Financial Decisions

Involving children in family financial discussions and decisions demystifies money matters and highlights the importance of financial planning. This engagement offers a practical understanding of managing finances and prepares them for future decision-making.

Conclusion

Teaching financial responsibility is a journey that begins with simple lessons in earning and saving and evolves into more complex topics like budgeting, debt management, and credit use. By starting these lessons early, we lay a strong foundation for our children's financial independence and success. As parents, our role is to guide, educate, and model the financial behaviors we hope to instill in our children, ensuring they grow into financially savvy adults.

Chapter 15: The Importance of Good Communication Skills and Listening

Good communication starts with active listening. It means taking the time to really understand what someone is saying, not just hearing the words they're speaking. It's about being fully present and engaged, not distracted by our own thoughts or agendas. Active listening shows that we respect and value the other person's perspective and that we're willing to take the time to hear them out.

As a youth football coach, I often see the impact of good communication and listening on the field. When our team is on the same page, we can execute plays more effectively, anticipate each other's moves, and adjust our strategy in real-time. When we communicate well, we build trust and cohesion, which translates into better teamwork and more successful outcomes.

But good communication isn't just important on the football field - it's essential in all aspects of life. In school, effective communication can help students build strong relationships with teachers, classmates, and administrators. It can also help them express their needs and advocate for themselves in the classroom.

As a father, I know that good communication skills can help my children build strong relationships with others and navigate life's challenges more effectively. When they learn to listen actively, express their thoughts and feelings clearly, and seek to understand others, they're more likely to build positive connections and avoid conflict.

So, how can we teach our kids good communication skills and listening? As a football coach, I use a few simple strategies that apply both on and off the field:

- Model good communication: Kids learn from our example, so it's important to model active listening and effective communication in our own interactions with them and with others.

- Create opportunities for practice: Whether it's through group discussions, role-playing, or other activities, giving kids opportunities to practice their communication skills in a safe and supportive environment can help them build confidence and fluency.

- Use teachable moments: Whenever conflicts or misunderstandings arise, take the time to talk through them with your child. Use these moments to model good communication skills and reinforce the importance of active listening and clear expression.

- Provide feedback: Let your child know when they're communicating effectively and offer specific feedback when they're not. Help them understand the impact of their words and actions on others and encourage them to make adjustments as needed.

Overall, good communication skills and listening are critical to success on the football field and in life. As a father and coach, I know that by teaching these skills to our children, we're setting them up for success and helping them build strong, positive relationships with others.

Chapter 16: How to Handle Stress and Cope With Difficult Situations

Equipping Children for Life's Challenges: A Parental Blueprint

Preparing children for the inevitable stresses and challenges of life is one of the most significant tasks we face as parents. While it's impossible to shield them completely, equipping them with the tools to manage stress with resilience is crucial.

Modeling Healthy Stress Management

Leading by Example

Children are observant learners. Demonstrating healthy stress management through self-care, setting boundaries, and maintaining our physical and mental health teaches them to emulate these practices.

Developing Coping Mechanisms

Encouraging Emotional Expression

Providing children with the means to express their feelings and manage stress is vital. Techniques can include mindfulness, breathing exercises, and other personalized coping strategies to navigate stressful situations.

Fostering Independence and Problem-Solving Skills

Encouraging Critical Thinking

As children encounter complex challenges, teaching them problem-solving skills and promoting critical thinking enhances their independence and self-reliance.

Emotional Regulation Skills

Managing Emotional Responses

Teaching children to recognize and regulate their emotions, as well as appropriately respond to others' feelings, is essential for personal and professional success.

Building Support Networks

Creating Connections

Helping children forge strong relationships with family, friends, and mentors ensures they have a supportive community for guidance and emotional support during tough times.

Embracing Life's Challenges

Normalizing Stress and Difficult Situations

Acknowledging that stress is a part of life and instilling resilience in children prepares them to face life's challenges head-on, equipped with the necessary skills and confidence.

By teaching our children these strategies, we provide them with a valuable toolkit to navigate life's stresses and challenges, fostering resilience, emotional intelligence, and independence that will benefit them throughout their lives.

Chapter 17: How to Apologize and Make Amends When Necessary

Fostering Accountability and the Art of Making Amends: A Father's Role

As a devoted father, one of the paramount lessons I strive to impart to my children is the significance of owning their actions and understanding how to sincerely apologize and rectify any harm caused. These abilities are crucial not just for their personal integrity and growth but also for enriching their relationships and bolstering their successes in life.

The Power of Apology and Making Amends

Enhancing Trust and Forgiveness

Research underscores the positive impacts of apologizing and making amends, noting that apologies can foster trust and forgiveness and reduce negative emotions for both the aggrieved and the apologizer. This mutual benefit highlights the transformative power of genuine apologies in healing and strengthening relationships.

Overcoming Challenges in Apologizing

Cultivating Vulnerability and Responsibility

Many individuals grapple with apologizing due to fears of vulnerability or feelings of shame and guilt. As fathers, we can guide our children through these challenges by exemplifying accountability and teaching them the following key steps:

Acknowledging Responsibility: It's crucial to admit wrongdoing and acknowledge the harm caused.

Offering a Sincere Apology: A genuine apology recognizes the impact on the aggrieved and expresses true remorse.

Making Amends: This may involve proposing a solution or inquiring what actions can help repair the relationship.

Following Through: Commitment to change and following through with promised actions are vital to truly mend the relationship.

Encouraging Continuous Growth

Commitment to Improvement

Apologizing and making amends aren't one-off solutions but a continuous journey toward personal development and relationship enhancement. Creating a supportive environment where children feel safe to express themselves and learn from their mistakes is essential.

The Role of Professional Support

Seeking Further Guidance

Encouraging children to seek professional help if needed can further support their journey in mastering these critical skills, enhancing their ability to navigate and mend complex relationships.

Impact on Professional Success

Building Trustworthiness and Credibility

Effective apology and amends-making skills are pivotal not only in personal relationships but also in professional contexts. Demonstrating accountability can lead to being perceived as more trustworthy and credible, facilitating positive career outcomes.

Conclusion

Teaching our children the importance of acknowledging their mistakes, apologizing sincerely, and making amends is a vital aspect of their development. By leading by example and fostering an environment conducive to open emotional expression and responsibility, we equip our children with the tools for building robust relationships and achieving success across all facets of their lives.

Chapter 18: How to Show Empathy and Compassion Towards Others

Nurturing Empathy and Compassion: A Father's Mission

In a world where empathy and compassion are more necessary than ever, as a father, I consider it my paramount duty to instill these values in my children. Empathy, the ability to understand and share the feelings of another, combined with compassion, the drive to alleviate others' suffering, form the cornerstone of meaningful human connections.

The Significance of Empathy and Compassion

Foundation for Positive Relationships

Teaching our children empathy and compassion from a young age lays the groundwork for stronger, healthier relationships. Such values deter negative behaviors like bullying, fostering a spirit of helpfulness and cooperation instead.

Benefits for Mental Health

Beyond benefiting others, empathy and compassion enrich our own lives, enhancing our sense of community and purpose. This connection can significantly reduce stress, anxiety, and depression, contributing to overall mental well-being.

Effective Strategies for Teaching Empathy and Compassion

Modeling Through Action

Children are astute observers, learning through our actions. Demonstrating empathy and compassion in our daily interactions serves as a powerful lesson for our children, showcasing the behavior we hope to see reflected in them.

Encouraging Emotional Expression and Understanding

Fostering an environment where children feel comfortable discussing their emotions and where we actively encourage them to consider others' feelings cultivates empathy. Questions like "How do you think that made your friend feel?" can prompt insightful discussions.

Practicing Active Listening

Teaching our children to listen attentively to others not only shows respect but also deepens their understanding and empathy. Encouraging them to ask questions and show genuine interest in others' experiences reinforces this learning.

Promoting Acts of Kindness

Encouraging children to perform acts of kindness, no matter how small, can have a profound impact. Simple gestures like holding a door or sharing a toy can teach the value of compassion.

Utilizing Stories and Media

Books and films that highlight empathy and compassion provide valuable teaching moments. Sharing these stories can spark conversations about understanding and helping others.

Volunteering as a Family

Engaging in volunteer work together offers practical experience in compassion, showing children the real-world impact of their actions and fostering a sense of social responsibility.

Conclusion

Instilling empathy and compassion in our children is not just about raising kind individuals; it's about contributing to a more empathetic and compassionate world. By leading by example, engaging in meaningful discussions, and providing opportunities for our children to practice empathy and compassion, we lay the foundation for a future marked by understanding and caring interactions. Let's commit to being role models of empathy and compassion, paving the way for our children to build a brighter, more connected future.

Chapter 19: The Importance of Setting and Achieving Goals

Empowering Children Through Goal-Setting: A Father's Perspective

As fathers, one of our essential roles is to guide our children in setting and achieving their goals. Goal-setting is a vital skill that lays the foundation for success in various life domains, from academics and sports to personal growth and career aspirations.

The Importance of Goal-Setting

- Why Set Goals?

- Direction and Purpose: Goals provide children with a clear direction, helping them focus on what is truly important and fostering a sense of purpose.

- Confidence Building: Achieving set goals boosts children's confidence, reinforcing their belief in their capabilities and encouraging them to embrace new challenges.

- Enhanced Motivation: Clear, attainable goals can significantly motivate children, propelling them forward and sustaining their efforts through visible progress.

- Skill Development: The process of goal-setting enhances planning and organizational skills, teaching children how to break tasks into manageable steps and strategize their path to success.

- Personal Growth: Pursuing goals demands resilience, effort, and adaptability, promoting personal development and preparing children for future challenges.

Supporting Your Child's Goal-Setting Journey

Practical Tips for Parents

- Foster a Goal-Setting Mindset: Initiate conversations about the value of goals, assisting your children in identifying and articulating their aspirations.

- Simplify Complex Goals: Guide your children in breaking down ambitious goals into smaller, achievable milestones, easing the path to accomplishment.

- Craft a Strategy Together: Collaborate with your children to outline a detailed plan for reaching their goals, including specific actions, deadlines, and checkpoints.

- Offer Steady Support: Provide consistent encouragement and support, celebrating milestones and offering constructive guidance through setbacks.

- Lead by Example: Demonstrate the power of goal-setting by pursuing and discussing your own goals inspiring your children through your actions and commitment.

The Science Behind Goal-Setting

- Empirical Evidence

- Research suggests that individuals who write down their goals are significantly more likely to achieve them compared to those who don't, underscoring the power of explicitly articulating objectives.

- Despite the low success rate of New Year's resolutions, the act of making explicit resolutions dramatically increases the likelihood of achievement.

- Setting specific, challenging goals is associated with enhanced performance, as specificity and difficulty level are critical factors in goal effectiveness.

- Goal-setting practices have been linked to reduced stress levels and improved well-being, highlighting their role in promoting mental health.

Conclusion

Instilling the practice of goal-setting in our children is not merely about achieving specific outcomes but about equipping them with a mindset and skills that will serve them throughout their lives. By supporting our children in setting, pursuing, and reflecting on their goals, we lay the groundwork for a lifetime of purposeful direction, personal growth, and resilience. As fathers, our engagement in this process is invaluable, offering guidance, encouragement, and an example to follow.

Chapter 20: How to Handle Conflicts and Disagreements

A Father's Blueprint for Nurturing Essential Life Skills

Fatherhood is a profound journey that transcends the mere act of parenting. It's about guiding our children through the complexities of life, instilling in them the virtues of empathy, integrity, perseverance, and the practicality of financial wisdom. Each lesson we impart is a step toward shaping them into well-rounded, responsible adults.

Teaching Conflict Resolution

The Cornerstone of Healthy Relationships

Conflict is an inevitable part of human interaction, but it's how we manage these disagreements that define the quality of our relationships. Teaching our children the art of conflict resolution—through active listening, emotional regulation, seeking common ground, and respectful communication—equips them with the tools for building and maintaining healthy relationships.

The Value of Active Listening and Emotional Management

Understanding and Respect

Active listening and managing emotions are critical in navigating conflicts constructively. By modeling active listening and demonstrating how to remain calm in the face of disagreement, we teach our children to approach conflicts with empathy and composure.

Fostering Empathy and Compassion

Building Connections

Empathy and compassion are vital for understanding and connecting with others. Encouraging our children to see the world from others' perspectives and to act with kindness strengthens their emotional intelligence and social bonds.

Instilling Integrity and Hard Work

The Foundation of Character

Integrity and a strong work ethic are essential for personal and professional success. By emphasizing the importance of honesty, responsibility, and perseverance, we lay the groundwork for our children to achieve their goals and lead meaningful lives.

Financial Literacy and Responsibility

Preparing for the Future

Teaching our children to manage money wisely, from budgeting to understanding debt, prepares them for financial independence and security. These lessons in fiscal responsibility are crucial for navigating the adult world.

The Journey of Fatherhood

Guidance, Support, and Love

While fatherhood comes without a manual, sharing our knowledge and experiences provides our children with a roadmap to navigate life's challenges. Our role is to offer guidance, support, and unconditional love, helping our children grow into compassionate, responsible adults.

Conclusion

with opportunities to teach, guide, and support our children. By instilling in them the values of empathy, integrity, perseverance, and financial Our prudence, we prepare them for the challenges and triumphs ahead. This blueprint for fatherhood is not about perfection but about the relentless pursuit of guiding our children toward their best selves journey as fathers is filled.

What makes "I Miss My Dad" uniquely compelling is its ability to speak directly to the soul of any father or son. The author's candid reflections on the trials and triumphs of fatherhood are interlaced with actionable strategies and supported by research findings, making this book an indispensable resource for fathers committed to fostering a lasting bond with their sons.

At its core, "I Miss My Dad" is a testament to the enduring significance of a father's influence. It challenges readers to reflect on the depth of this connection, offering solace, inspiration, and a call to action for fathers to embrace their pivotal role in guiding their sons toward becoming compassionate, resilient, and ethical leaders of tomorrow.

This book is more than a collection of parenting advice—it is a heartfelt invitation to acknowledge the transformative power of fatherhood and embark on a journey of intentional parenting. Whether you're rekindling your relationship with your son or laying the groundwork for a lifetime of understanding and mutual respect, "I Miss My Dad" offers timeless wisdom and the practical tools you need to navigate the complexities of raising a son in today's world.

Prepare to be moved, challenged, and inspired as "I Miss My Dad: The Importance of a Father in a Son's Life" unveils the profound legacy of fatherhood. This book is not merely a guide—it's a beacon for those seeking to build a future enriched with love, strength, and integrity for their sons.

About the Author

Brian K. Smith: Entrepreneur, Content Creator, Author, and Inspirational Coach

As an entrepreneur alongside Monica, my wife of 18 years, I co-operate a thriving limousine service and a salon. My foray into content creation led to the establishment of a YouTube channel, THE CONFIDENCE COACH, where I impart wisdom and encouragement.

My educational background includes graduating from Perry Traditional Academy in 1989 and attending the University of Pittsburgh from 1989 until 1993. I further enriched my understanding of human behavior with a course in criminal psychology in 2004.

Currently, I serve as a coach and board member for the Westside Mustangs Youth Football Organization and actively participate in Macedonia Baptist Church. These roles allow me to make a meaningful impact in my community, especially among the youth.

I am passionately committed to teaching young people about the endless possibilities available to them and firmly believe in the critical importance of strong family structures for achieving success.

My mission is to instill in everyone I encounter the belief that everything they need already exists within them. I advocate for the power of belief and the ability to achieve anything we can dream of, as long as we have faith in our potential.

Made in the USA
Middletown, DE
22 August 2024

59007817R00051

Empower

Publishing

Mom Murphy's

Treasured Recipes

By

Frances Krites Murphy

Empower Publishing
Winston-Salem

Empower

Publishing

Empower Publishing
PO Box 26701
Winston-Salem, NC 27114

First Empower Publishing Books edition published
November, 2016
Empower Publishing, Feather Pen, and all production design are trademarks.

For information regarding bulk purchases of this book, digital purchase and special discounts, please contact the publisher at empowerpublishing2015@gmail.com

Cover design by Pan Morelli

Manufactured in the United States of America
ISBN 978-1540816481